WHO IS RESPONSIBLE

FOR UNIVERSE AND OUR PROBLEMS

-ONE QUESTION THAT EVERY POOR CHILD ASKS.
-ONE QUESTION TO UNDERSTAND THE MYSTERY OF LIFE.
-ONE QUESTION THAT WILL LEAD TO THE PATH OF SUCCESS.

RAVINDRA VAISHNAV

BlueRose ONE.com
Stories Matter

First Published in March 2022

ISBN: 978-93-93809-42-1

BLUEROSE PUBLISHERS

www.bluerosepublishers.com

info@bluerosepublishers.com

+91 8882 898 898

Cover Design:

Akash

Typographic Design:

Namrata Saini

Distributed by: BlueRose, Amazon, Flipkart

Our world is amazing and mysterious. So much so that even failure brings opportunities with it, just our condemnation keeps us deprived of its correct use.

-Ravindra Vaishnav

Contents

Words of mind

My life in itself is weird and surprising.

In many ways sometimes I feel whatever has happened in my life against my will has opened the doors of success and growth but sometimes I'm nothing more than an unsuccessful, poor, and unlucky person.

Many people hide their real personalities.

I don't know what they presume about themselves, but I think accepting your reality is like passing the first step towards change.

You require courage and confidence for this.

Usually, people take the death of another person courageously but they don't even get a thought in their dreams of dying themselves.

And then one day death arises and men don't come out of their pretty world of dreams and imagination and have to bid final goodbye to the world.

what is life in reality, what is growth called, what kind of a life can be called a successful life, questions like this keep on pondering in my mind because if you look at this world it's nothing more than the crowd of dead people and you can't expect cooperation, smartness, and intelligence from dead people!

A dead person can do nothing more than exploitation, repression, and violence and this is happening all around the world today.

The human species have the most powerful things like wealth, developed machines, and spectacular scientists' knowledge.

Apart from a group of people, everyone is deprived of these resources just because they don't have the penny to spend.

Is money that important?

Can't this world work without monetary resources?

Or do we require new management that is based on the hard work of the person instead of using money?

So that hard work and wealth are divided equally and the society of thieves and criminals vanishes.

I can't certainly tell what would be the future of humans but with the help of my experience and knowledge, I can surely say that numerous talents, brilliance, and individuality have been targeted because of this shortcoming.

And we all know how people wrongfully use their power.

The most difficult procedure is that of improving.

because until the revolutionary level changes from the mental level to the practical level, then there will be an empire of money in our society. And as long as earning is part of a person's life till then all kinds of wrongful and rightful things will keep on happening in our society.

The reason behind writing this book is to awaken the people towards life and understand and know what is the ultimate reality? What is spirituality and how can they attain the real happiness of life? I understand the value of money but if I keep my motive to be only rich then no one is foolish than me.

Human life is an incredible journey if you choose the right path you can go from having nothing to having everything with dignity.

We have endless possibilities of progress inside us but it is necessary to be awakened towards it.

If we give up our narrow visions and look at the actual ground if we keep on walking on the paths told by others to us for our selfishness until then it is not possible to reach the right destination till our last moments because that way goes nowhere who's traveler is adjourned.

And the truth is instead of walking on the life path almost every human has stopped at substantial wealth.

I hope after reading this book your life will have a new perspective, and you will have a better capability of understanding the problems and finding their solutions.

But above that, I hope that your inner soul will be awakened and that will not only scent your life but also of those who will come in your contact.

Your well-wisher,

Ravindra Vaishnav

Kailash Nagar, Sanchore (343041)

Jalore, Rajasthan.(India)

Chapter 1:

Importance of human life

1. we are special-

This world is full of different kinds of species and creatures. Life inhibits everywhere from sea to sky. The incredibility of life can be seen when the dry and barren desert where it becomes impossible to stay even for a few hours. Life exists forever there as well. In my view, people of the desert are an example of the struggle in life, in which snakes and lizards have inhibited the natural surroundings so much so that they can survive without the drop of water for their whole lives.

Apart from this, some desert plants do not receive water from the roots but develop from the spring dew. These traits are not common, they are developed over the crores of years. But despite all these traits, these whole defeats, there is no creature with intelligence and progress who is ahead of humans. Human development is so fast and unique that from this we can understand that there is something special about it. This cannot only be called natural development.

Because of nature's development, despite all possibilities, the rest of the organisms considering how fast and mysterious the progress of human civilization has been, it's clear that there is something special within us. This cannot be termed as a natural progression, because nature has given equal opportunities to other life forms to progress too. development is special in a special direction is the indication of the presence of elements.

If you analyze one person, you will find the package of sensations, concepts, and available information but these qualities are found in animals as well. The only difference is they use these qualities based on the situations around them.

Animals use the resources according to the situation and their situations are satisfied by food, shelter, and sense gratification or can be called suitable circumstances. On the other hand, a human is filled with the feelings like greediness, ego, jealousy, love, and many numerous feelings which insist him to do the rightful things sometimes and the wrongful the other time.

Somewhere the reason for this variegated progress of the human race is this feeling of sympathy.

But some people have separated themselves from the world and have opted for revolutionary life and in return, they have explored scientific revolutions for the humans on which our lives are surviving and we can't even imagine their non-existence.

Just think of electricity, mobile phones, digital engines that didn't exist then how this world would have been. It is because of these uncountable knowns and unknown inventors and discoverers surpassing contributions for human beings that we can reach the doormat of this unparalleled progress.

The creatures of earth behave according to the excessive progress of nature, we rarely can see humans acting against their natural behavior. While humans from the start are born with the qualities that make them act differently from similar behavior.

Humans break the instinctive law as no species can do suicide as humans can. Like this, every creature has a doomsday but a human is an animal that does not have a fixed doomsday. We can find uncountable examples that hint towards the unique powers mankind has and he can reach this stature of success whereas it's another topic to discuss how mankind has made his life hell.

2. An Unstoppable War

If you barrel a bag full of one thousand dollars in a center of the market, people will be head over heels for each other, and in this snatching and pillaging some might even die.

This is what is happening in real life.

For what, for whom, and how much is required? No one asks these questions now. Everyone is just blindly fighting. Those who are powerful and potentially viable are killing and those who are weak are getting killed.

But no one is giving up!

The limitless hunger of winning this unstoppable war has ruined human civilization. It has desolated millions of lives and god knows how many more families it's going to destroy.

In many ways, wealth is the need of human beings but somewhere in reality it has become the servant of the trap of unstoppability and we can't see a solution to this problem. Whomever you look at, they turn fifteen to twenty years old, and the question of living and giving life has been asked to die.

There is only one mindset of these young minds i.e. what I want is what I want, if I don't get it I will snatch it.

This situation is serious and scary and what is more difficult is its solution because human beings are emotional creatures that is why they have not accepted the monetary difference between rich and poor and they should not even accept it. After all, it is an immoral thing as mammon and an institute given by science have been acquired by a small number of people based on a piece of paper and they have taken its full authority.

Everyone, even the animals have an equal right to the present wealth on this earth. But unluckily humans consider themselves fortunate enough and instead of sharing everything they enjoy the pitiful situation of those who are hungry and fulfill their egos. Kingdoms of these people live till they meet a woke individual and when this happens, a gruesome conflict happens.

Today whatever is happening in society is an example of this conflict only and it is possible as well. A defeated man may leave his sense of identifying right and wrong. This situation leads to crimes, murders, theft, and whatnot. We have to accept the truth that every crime has a specific reason behind it. There is a lot of science on it.

And a criminal is created either because of the culmination of distress or size of drenched majesty or absence of uselessness because many times person in the presence of propitious situation around him becomes so careless and irresponsible that he neither care even a bit about the emotions of people around him nor he is aware of the problems of fellow beings.

Look at people who are from rich families and somewhat belong to this group of society. Just like common criminals, the government does not have the power to punish these rich people.

And what happens in the four-walled palace is known to none.

Altogether, the reality is when resources are limited and people wishing for their procurement are more till then this unstoppable war is going to happen.

But in the present scenario, resources are not limited to some level. If food, shelter, clothes, etc are distributed after measuring then everyone's needs can be fulfilled with the available amount of resources.

But against this, it does not seem that in this war it's nothing apart from the crowd of blinds snatching and snapping.

3. Your Thoughts Are The Foundation Of Your Personality

A common man is neither silent nor thinks ahead of his daily living needs.

In this world, 99% of the population spend their life according to a fixed daily life routine, which results in the majority of people not seeing and realizing the world inside them, their capabilities, and actual supreme truth.

What is the actual supreme truth?

We will try to understand this with a basic example. I'll tell you a real incident from my life.

Once upon a time, I was going from a street in Bangalore, suddenly I saw an extremely aged and poor lady catch my eye. For her it was difficult to even handle her own body, she was so feeble that her neck was shivering even if she was looking here and there.

I went towards her, and at that time I only had ₹20 in my pocket, nothing else I could do to help her.

And I helped her according to my capacity.

In reality, at that time if I had ₹50,000 in my pocket I would have given that wholesome amount to her because she needed that money.

And in the end at this age, she is not earning enough money to buy a Mercedes.

She was just sitting there to earn enough to have two meals. And many people were going from that street. Many big millionaires were going there. But no one took notice of her. And some were giving her sly looks. This is the ultimate reality. We have to accept that nothing is ours.

Whatever is there will stay here only and whatever is available for us we should use it in the best way to prove that we deserve it. When nothing wrong happened to me after giving ₹20 to that poor old lady then it won't be a harm to rich people as well.

But they don't have a glimpse of reality.

For them the explanation and definition of the world is nothing more than me and unto me.

For any human being, no reality can be as scary as this one, and because of this, there is a lack of concern.

If we keenly and closely look at the scenario then we can see till the moments ago when it was a worrisome situation. We will see this opportunity only, the one opportunity that can change everything inside and outside of you but it requires universal awareness.

Thought is a word full of qualities and secrets and no one in the human race inspires humans towards ideological revolution.

From Christ to Buddha and Osho, the greatest magnificent people acquired by the earth, their motive always was to somehow show the way of emancipation to the people of hell.

But against this, humans are so egoistic and cavalier of themselves that instead of walking on the right path they torture others who are on the right path.

They try every possible way to prove the truth a lie and to announce greed, solicitation, craving, and amours as the correct way of living.

If you look at today's world, especially the people of the western world, they are flourished with indulgent attitudes and we can't see any possible redressal for this.

It's not that I don't support a happy life, instead, I believe that every human should be given equal wealth on this earth but everything is happening contrarily.

Some are dying by binge eating and some are dying by starvation.

The main reason behind this differentiation is that humans have accepted the reality they have been told. They didn't make any efforts to step down from the laps of nature and investigate.

4. Choose The Highest Aim In Life

When I used to study in school, my teacher used to repetitively say this, you all should study hard and if you score well then you can become a doctor or engineer, you will be renowned and you will earn a lot of money.

Everything is good. It's not wrong to become a doctor or engineer nor is it wrong to earn a lot of money.

But is there any aim of life higher than this?

Is there any work from which you can earn something more valuable than money?

In this matter, my classmates were not so lucky but I was. I always knew that the aim of my life should be bigger than money. Because there are uncountable people who are millionaires and after seeing this real scene we can only say that money only satisfies the ego of human beings. Inner peace and happiness have no relation with this at all.

Once your heart accepts the real revelation was doing but once you give up the wish of money and wealth or any profit and choose then the result itself will be glorious and by walking on this route you might now earn any benefit from the worldly perspective but you will experience a commendable change of your soul that you will feel free every time.

In my case, if you ask, I have such an experience that if I die at this moment then neither I will be having any complaint from anyone nor I have any work or motive that would motivate me to live more.

Because your lifelong wish gets fulfilled when the universe appears itself. When I have understood the tale of descendants now I have no interest in this ongoing drama.

And even don't have any kind of connection towards it. Because on the matter of vision the visionary is the basis itself as you can't see the vision with lack of visionary.

We can understand with some effort. – a common man might not understand. But this is the ultimate reality.

In our society especially India, a wholesome number of the population is deprived of basic services and resources and they are living a very difficult and painful life. On the dynamic level, it is better but as we look at the urban population's life it is difficult to believe that God's given life could be like this. And on the other hand, the reality we see is that life is not a gift but for some people, it is not less than punishment and nothing more.

Such situations did not come in the future, from parents to teachers and the whole society tries to emphasize one thought in the mind of kids that money is life and earning money is the only target of life.

In situations like this, it is difficult to arrive at a decision that should be given more importance whether the high ideals or anyhow earned money. Because humans have created management like that wealth is life only. High ideals are not important.

That is the big reason that today social crime is at its peak. People have lost sensations and all of the things are happening that should not happen. The wonder is when we look at the Indian theaters.

It shows nothing more than the cheap mentality of cheap actors. And those people are cheaper than those who waste both of their time and money to watch such movies.

People like these are a problem for a country because it resulted in for today's youth a hero who is a drunk, thug, or characterless lost person dancing on the roads. A person wants to progress, equality and for this, the path he chooses makes him like this hero.

It is obvious there is nothing on this path apart from failures and it is also turning into reality in the current times.

Apart from a small group of people, no one is successful and satisfied. The whole universe is lacking the high and correct aim and walking towards destruction.

Chapter 2

The formula of a successful life

1. Who Is Successful?

I don't consider a person successful who is senseless, who is dead, and who does not know how to practice life estates. Money, position, prestige, and capacity can be someone else measures but the person who doesn't know who even himself. Who is walking in a mob mentality and who sees what is shown to him. A person like this cannot be called successful despite having a lot of money. Not in our society, in fact in the whole world, the meaning of success is changing. And people who do not know the value of love, service, and cooperation.

The meaning of success is having the talent to complete our work in hand with happiness and when there is no way, to build our way to reaching our aim. Only based on money and material achievements, a decision of success cannot be taken. If we look at the world's self-respected and the greatest saints, we will get to know that they were unsuccessful in general things. But because of their skills and correct planning, they were able to do revolutionary work in their lives. The things that the present rich of that time were not able to do being material less they were able to do the most important things in life.

Those people were honest successful people and their lives were successful lives. Maybe the reality is only that till the time people like Chanakya are silent the fools are safe and ruling. They can even destroy wealthy people.

Sometimes money is with the fools and those who keep it safe are the greatest fools. Greatest fools because they know that the materialized cannot be taken with us but despite the fact, the precious life is spent to collect money are the greatest fools only. It won't take time for their ancestral wealth to vanish.

One great fool dies after dedicating his life to collecting useless things and the other fool follows him. Fool dies by spending his wealth earned without any hard work or experience in buying the unnecessary things. This is the reality of most of the rich families. And this cannot be called success.

2. Success Is Beneath, Not Outside:-

Despite hard work, ability, and intelligence most people are still unsuccessful and indifferent to society. Even with the status of pride, greed, and so on the bad life is not even enjoyed yet it is the reckless and noisy environment that is created.

If the journey of success is started properly then we will get to know that it begins with the inner change. To know your mistakes and correct them is the first and foremost step. Without that nobody gets success to date and if they would have then it would not be for a longer time.

This is a very common and usual thing that humans don't know about themselves. How will he judge the outer world and the way of working?

And lack of correct information results in wrong destinations.

If it's looked carefully, we can see that the people who speak less and work with patience, work is appreciable enough to hold up a good position and that can increase their chance of success.

It is important to understand yourself and accept the power that stops you from doing every such task which is charitable. Why is it so that in every task we look for a personal benefit? Once we recognize and accept the demonic power that affects us this way, the next important task at hand is to have the bravery to walk a path against this power and destroy its influence upon you. This is because fear and greed in us are two such qualities that are the biggest enemies of peace, tranquility, and success. Their presence alone gives birth to imaginative and unnecessary courses of action, which can result in the downfall of even the greatest people.

In reality the peace and tranquility, we look for in the outside world or try to get by money is present inside us all along. We only need to see and accept the truth and break the barriers that keep us in the dark, the barriers of greed and mortal pleasures, which we have imposed on ourselves.

3. Meaning Of Failure

Failure also has its various - good and helpful meanings. When in life, a decision at the right time gives the wrong results, then the result isn't just a loss but also a lesson, a very important experience is at hand. This lesson if used well then can help avoid even bigger losses in the future. Experience is the type of knowledge that holds the power to guarantee success in any kind of circumstances. A simple example is that a driver who travels along the same route every day, knows very well every bump and curve on the road, however, a driver new to the route doesn't hold any experience of it and the result is that in case he makes a mistake, it results in an accident, which is a common event.

This explains clearly the value of experience gained from a failure, it plays an important role in the events that are supposed to happen in the future. It may be possible that while doing something for the first time you may not have enough or correct information and you might fail. But the second time your experience will be helpful and the probability of your success is improved for sure.

Along with experience failure also brings along with it sadness.

Anger and disappointment. Which is a test of your endurance and patience. If you learn to face these problems with positivity and self-confidence then the level of your power to persevere through hardships increases so much that it becomes very difficult for negativity and self-doubt to cloud your judgment in the future. Moreover, self-confidence is among the most important prerequisites for success.

Aside from experience and self-confidence, another usual requirement to achieve success and learn valuable lessons is the ability of a person to accept their own mistakes. If we look at it deeply, most of the failures in life are due to the wrong perception of reality and the acts done on the imagination or wrong predictions of the person. A typical person can find a thousand things wrong with the circumstances or other people but find it impossible to accept that they lacked a certain skill to be able to succeed. Accepting your mistakes and improving on them is a must to achieve success in life, and if we look at it deeply, the opportunities to learn and the lessons we get from our mistakes and failures are rarely offered or known even by the greatest of teachers and guides. And even if they knew, it is impossible to teach these things to anyone else. Thus, at least in my experience, failure often brings much to us, it just matters how much we can keep with us.

4. Never betray yourself

The difference between deeds and goals is one such shortcoming that is found in 99 percent of the population. In some capacity, this is one of the reasons why most of the population have failed and a small group of people has become the owners of most of the wealth of the entire world. However, not all rich people are deserving or talented, some are so untalented and useless that it is almost impossible to believe they could ever acquire such wealth. But still, such undeserving people are deemed successful in the eyes of the world. This is a matter we will further discuss later.

If we look at the past and these conditions, then we can appreciate the wonders of the internet, the success stories of which fill every corner of the world. From the greatest world leaders to the unknown poets, everyone in some way or form presents their success, gratefulness, etc and millions of people read such thoughts. Upon experiencing such an environment filled with great thoughts it feels like everyone has a great spirit like that of the Buddha present inside them. But unfortunately, the reality is much different from this. I wouldn't like to say much. This hypocrisy of preaching something else and doing something else, nothing can be more dangerous for any human who wants to live a better life.

It is important to understand that to consider a life successful, it has to be more than a life just limited to money. A person whose deeds fall short of what he preaches, gets his opinion disrespected and his future destroyed. Such a man is neither capable of loving someone, nor is he deserving of someone else's love. However low someone can fall in my opinion, it can never be lower than a person who doesn't live up to his words. Such a hypocrite should be treated less than even an animal.

From a realistic point of view, more or less, this shortcoming is present in all of us somewhere. Maybe we are still deprived and unaware of the power that the great spirits of Buddha and Mahavir got, or the feeling a truly selfless person gets from bringing a smile to someone's face. Because to drown someone who knows how to swim, even the center of an ocean might not be enough but to drown someone who doesn't know how to swim, even a small pond is enough. Any person who claims to walk the path of dharma, knowledge, and buddha and says he got nothing for it, is for sure a liar. Because people who have walked this path have gotten everything and those who don't have the determination to walk this path shouldn't expect to gain anything from it. Because

For such a person to drown and fail is part of the arrangement of nature itself.

Within our world, there are as many little worlds as there are humans. Just like how a poor person spends the night on the pavement while another rich man spends the night in their manor. Even though these 2 people live in the same world their worlds are far apart. Rarely is someone able to cross the distance and cut the disparities between these worlds, the power, and rights of most who die in the world where they were born? Now, this has been and will be unknown forever, as to who gets to decide the people who live in the comfort of palaces or who is supposed to live a life of labor and suffering. Because the cruel reality is that intelligence and hard work barely matter when you are born in a poor household. At least these things don't matter until the time you learn to walk on your own two feet. And I have seen even little kids working as manual labor, the kids who are naïve enough to not even know who the man stamped on every note is.

A person betrays the truth concerning other people then it results in such situations. Not only in this country but in every part of this world there are such disgraceful youths whose lives don't amount to anything and they somehow just scrape by fulfilling the hunger of their desire. A beggar will give birth to a beggar. It doesn't matter how hardworking and talented the child is for at least 10 to 15 years of life, he will have to live in the circumstances in which his parents gave birth to him. Whether it's cold or hot, hunger or thirst nothing is in his control. For a child, his God is his father alone and a father's failure, or when a failure becomes a father, then, in my opinion, it results in the world's most unfortunate and sad circumstances. And the reason for this is only that somewhere someone betrayed themselves and despite having the truth in front of them chose to go down the wrong path.

5. Develop the power of acceptance

For any situation, protest, transformation or conversion and trying is the first step. But even before protest acceptance is first and foremost the most important and needed aspect to tackle any situation. There are many such examples where even influential and rich businessmen have become bankrupt and have gone from being at the top of the world to the pavements. If we investigate the reasons behind such downfalls then a major reason which arises is that these people failed to accept reality and instead denied believing what was happening to them. On one side their businesses were drowning in debt of billions and the salary of their workers was due for months. And on the other side, they spent extravagantly on lavish parties and expensive feasts.

Due to this in the end all that could happen was the absolute destruction of their wealth.

It is very common knowledge that in case of an earthquake it is best to run to a safe place but if you believe the opposite and deny that there is an earthquake at all and refuse to leave your bed, then your bed may serve as your coffin. Because the earthquake doesn't care if you believe in its existence or not, it will still be as destructive as it plans to be. It's a matter of self discretion that you accept it.

I don't know why sometimes the human mind becomes such a slave to the imagination that it loses touch with reality entirely, everything which happens to him seems to him as only imagination and his imaginative world seems the most real to him. And in his imagination what the person thinks of himself is difficult to imagine as well. But unfortunately, reality and imagination are complete opposites of each other and due to this many are destroyed, the relationships of many are broken and many protest so hard against the reality that to continue living in their imaginative world they end their real life.

6. Develop your self-confidence

For a successful life, self-confidence plays the most important role. Even if you have everything but don't have the confidence to do something, then there is not much you can achieve.

Self-confidence doesn't mean the habit to do anything whether right or wrong but the ability to predict the outcome of the task at hand appropriately before undertaking it. In this world, almost every step forward contains a new secret, and self-confidence is the key to deciphering all these secrets. It is not guaranteed that you may succeed every time but even in such conditions, the power to persevere is the only way to achieve success. Thousands of years ago humans fought for various resources and wealth with swords, shields, and countless other weapons. But today the world isn't at war in any visible form but every human fights for wealth and resources every day in an invisible form. From a simple vegetable vendor to the CEOs of companies with immeasurable wealth, everyone has to fight for their existence and to make the circumstances suitable to them. Thus, self-confidence mustn't break at any moment.

The second aspect of self-confidence is power, patience, and stability. A person with a peaceful mind and those who have patience are people who can fight for longer than others and persevere for longer as well. This is the quality that ensures achieving the goal because everyone else in the race will get tired and give up but those who last till the end will win.

Today's world is so difficult to live in that it is impossible to achieve anything by walking down a straight path. One such developed and powerful breed has evolved from our civilization that the weak and incapable people die-off of hunger and illness alone and no one is even there to ask about their well-being. These situations are very horrifying, and somewhere inside them every human is scared for themselves and wishes that they never get into such circumstances. It is necessary to remain careful but to be fearful is wrong because fear reduces the chances of our success and reduces our power to fight. There is only one solution to this: you believe in yourself and maintain self-control no matter the situation.

Chapter 3

An unfavorable situation is bound to come

1. The world is susceptible to change

The history of the earth is filled with rare secrets and mysteries, but the history of this universe is far more mysterious and filled with much greater secrets. How did it come into existence, how did matter form, how big is the space around us, etc are some of the many existential questions which can't be answered accurately even now and these secrets are unlikely to be uncovered even in the future. There are countless theories and some even have proof to confirm them but all in all the only real truth that can be extracted from these is that no one knows anything for sure. The only thing that can be agreed upon however is that the universe is not stable. It is constantly changing and growing. The borders of the universe are spread far and wide, and there is constantly destruction and new creation taking place within them, even if this isn't happening the universe has never been stable and the possibility of it being stable will never arise.

When even after billions and trillions of years, matter in this universe has not found stability, then how naïve can a human be to think he has achieved everything in life and he won't have to face the adversities of life, just because he has collected a bunch of pieces of paper or has gained a bit of respect and holds some influence in society.

To lead a wakeful life filled with awareness it is important to accept the truth that a king of today can be a beggar of tomorrow and the poorest of the poor can become among the richest overnight. It is important to accept this fact

That no matter how good life gets you should never let your grip on reality or the truth go below a certain point. Because the higher you get, the tighter your grip should be. Even a small mistake can become the difference between life and death.

A man who thinks of himself as the best in the world gets ravaged by the wheel of change so savagely that even the best can't help but panic by the change of circumstances. Firstly the mental and emotional power and perseverance get destroyed and secondly the outside situations prey on you. A person who is ready to fight is still better off but on the other hand, those who aren't ready for it get nothing but destruction. It is not the case that in such cases there is no other solution in such situations, but the solution can only be found by the people who have a wakeful and aware mind. And the problem is that nature often throws that person into the water who doesn't know how to swim. I don't understand why but in my experience destiny always preys on the weak, and the strong aren't spared the troubles either but it seems that the weak are always the ones who are affected the worst.

Nature and its powers might not be visible or tangible but its powers are a millionfold greater than those of even the most powerful and influential presidents. And due to this power even after countless such events where life should've been wiped out, it still thrives in full force.

Animals and birds have one favorable quality: they don't have to do anything to satisfy their egos. However, on the other hand, most humans act with a single goal of being the best. A very small minority of people live life with simple intentions and believe in a higher logic or enlightened thoughts. It is not bad to have ambition and neither is it bad to dream of being the world's richest person, but it is important to think deeply about if your dreams of success are resulting in someone's downfall. Even if people keep this in mind, according to me it is enough to make your life successful. Because the biggest mistake made by most people is that while chasing their dreams they get used to crossing some limits such as fraud,cheating is still okay, some people even paint their hands with blood. And usually, those who start their journey looking for light are left in darkness themselves. You can fool humans or the system but not nature, this is an important thing for everyone to realize.

2. The relationship between creation and destruction

Even if we investigate ten years of our life then we will realize the countless relationships that were left behind and the countless that were created. Step by step as life progresses, the old relationships may suffer and new relationships continue to be formed. Similarly, bad fortune and loss lay the foundation for a new beginning and set into motion an array of better things. Because nature believes in creation, it's not just humans but even a deer who barely escapes the fangs of a tiger runs with all his energy towards a new life. The matter of curiosity is what is the mysterious force that is creating such a strong will to live in the deer and giving it the power to escape death. The answer to this will be given by various people according to their perspectives but according to me nature's power of creation is such that whether it be a deer or a man on verge of death, this power can generate the will to live in any creature and give it immense power. Because nature knows that creation gives birth to death and only after death can a new birth take place.

In reality, humans are just animals. But unlike other animals, humans are more intelligent, which is why we have gotten ourselves into a lot of mess. And these are so complex that from a mental and emotional perspective even a man who earns millions a month won't look satisfied. Then what else can be expected from those who merely earn ten to fifteen thousand a month?

This is such a situation where every person feels as if they are going towards impending doom. Someone who is aware and has peace with himself knows what life is about or why we face ups and downs in life. This world would be a better place but I don't understand why a man who is struggling with life will put more effort into dragging others down instead of trying to get himself up. Some people who have struggled or faced sorrows due to lies and deceit of others, adopt the same behavior for dealing with other people, the kind of behavior they don't find acceptable towards themselves. And the feeling which supports such behavior is that if you want to save yourself from getting hurt then you have to hurt others.

I think that there is no simpler solution to destruction than this. Or to put it simply, you reap what you sow.

3. Where is rejection important

Change and better circumstances are only possible where there is protest or rejection. Because accepting things as there are isn't always beneficial. Because in difficult times, a man has to decide at his discretion where to speak and where not to. The protest or rejection of lies and injustice is always important. If nature rains suffering to such an extent that you can't even get enough to eat and sleep, then for once you can make friends and accept death and misery. But never stand with those who disrespect you and deal with you unjustly.

Wrong time and arrangements with wrong people can force you into such bad circumstances, that you will regret trying to get out of your other troubles through dealing with such people or walking on this path. You would wish that you had developed the perseverance to go through your previous troubles. Usually, people make the big mistake of creating more troubles while trying to get out of their current troubles. This is a kind of exploitation, the benefit of it is taken by everyone. Our system and society have developed such that usually there is the exploitation of the weak and they are made even weaker, and the strong get even more wealthy and powerful by reaping the benefits of this exploitation.

This is a very scary and dangerous situation and those who have accepted this, the children of such people find themselves stuck in this situation even though it wasn't their choice. From manual laborers to factory workers and every such person who earns a living wage by daily work finds themselves stuck in this situation where they feel all of their rights were taken away just because they were born in a poor household.

it is very difficult to find a way out of it. But the ways out of such a situation are very limited and not for the common people but those with more enlightened thoughts. There is an important role in many things from self-confidence to inner awareness and the approval nature. And even more important than this is the willpower of the person. In reality, most people don't want to live their life. For them, this world is only limited to being a means to satisfy their body and ego. The result of which is that they never try to do anything in life. All they do is to pass the days somehow. For example, If you give a drunk one crore rupees to start a business, he will go and spend them all on drugs, trying to get high. Not once will his brain come up with the thought of earning something using that money. He never hopes for growth in life, all he cares about is getting high and somehow will find a way to get high. Such people never rejected alcohol or drugs at all.

All in all the reality is that whenever a man ponders upon his problems with inner awareness and self-control then the path to the solution opens up automatically.

If a man is jailed for 2 years after being committed to a crime then the best solution is that he calms himself down for 2 years instead of trying to break out of prison. Because he could break out of prison and run away but he will never find independence by following this path. Such situations arise in everyone's life, whether rich or poor. Thus we should always decide with patience. It is not worth taking a huge loss in the future for a few short-term benefits.

Chapter 4

The reality of human civilization

Usually whenever we hear or read about such people who have achieved a high status in our society then we often notice them repeating the same thing that this life is a gift of God; you shouldn't let the invaluable time you get go to waste. But on the other hand when we think about the universe then we realize that it is filled with a tonne of problems and if you look closely no one wants to waste time on the contrary most people want to end their life right now. To most people life is far from a gift, it is more of a burden that someone has forced upon them and they are supposed to bear this burden for some time. All that can be seen everywhere are poverty, famine, and illness. Even some people who do look happy and healthy have become senseless and their hunger for wealth has grown so much that they aren't even aware of the people they are pushing to suffer and die in their race for money. The thing that surprises me the most is that there are still people claiming that human civilization is a developed civilization. The reality is that there are no other species as savage as humans on this earth because no member of any other species is pushed to the limits of suicide, no animal goes through the pain of having been raped by their fellow creatures and no animal is forced to starve unless there is a lack of a food source for the entire community.

The wonders of human civilization are that if you don't have the money you won't get access to food even though there is food literally rotting in shops and warehouses. If you want to see people dying off of hunger, visit Africa or read the history of the world wars. This experience will be enough to make you understand that there is no animal more savage than humans on this earth.

This behavior of humans is a deeply worrying matter. There are many reasons behind this and one by one we will discuss all such reasons

1. The human mindset and behavior

If you are asked who you are then you will probably start giving the description of your name, your mother's and father's name, and other details about your residence, nationality, etc. This is all well and good but if someone asks what you are then what would be your answer?

Human beings are nothing but a collection of emotions, thoughts, beliefs, and memories. In reality, 90 percent of people don't realize that they aren't living life by their standards or choices but unknowingly they are just walking the path which they are guided onto by others.

And this belief becomes so strong that people's faith in their path doesn't sway even if they have to kill someone or they come on the verge of death themselves. Because if this wasn't the case why would someone get happiness out of infiltrating another country and killing innocent people who he never even saw?

90 percent of the blame for most of our problems goes towards this misplaced faith and behavior only. Most people never think about whether the path they have chosen is right or wrong but instead, continue to follow the path they were shown as a child. For example, think about the mental state and development of a child growing up in a non-vegetarian family and a vegetarian family. It is obvious that there won't be much love or concern towards animals in a non-vegetarian family. However on the other hand the children of the vegetarian family would show much more concern and care towards the animals. Both of these perspectives aren't what the children made themselves, instead these are the ones they adopted by seeing the people around them. These perspectives only formed within the children because of the situation and circumstances in which these children were born and raised. If you look deeply even at the evilest people you will realize that humanity does exist within them if they got their mother's love in their childhood. Mostly you will notice that criminals grow up in such households where their mother and father might have died and these children suffer a lot from their childhood only.

A person who can ask questions has more chances to understand the situation and finds it easier to find the real truth. Their decision power and their capability to deal with the problems in their life are more enhanced as compared to others. Because whenever they are faced with any difficulty or they are asked to choose 1 path from a set of alternatives, then due to their self-confidence and willpower they are able to make the correct decision. Because of their inherent nature to question things they will always investigate the person giving the alternatives about who he is and once you know who the person guiding you is you can easily decide whether opting for the path suggested by that person would be beneficial or not. It is very important that our conscious element is active or no matter how many questions we ask we will end up down the path set out by our parents, teachers, and society and it isn't necessary that this path would be the correct one or that their beliefs about your life are correct.

Terrorism is a huge problem in our world and every year thousands of people die because of it. Countless nations have been ruined because of it and many are still forced to live in poverty and oppression. People living in normal and peaceful nations won't be able to understand the gravity of the situation, but many people suffer immensely because of terrorism, they lose their families, their homes and are even forced out of their nations.

This is a very concerning matter that a human is so set on killing another human just because they belong to different religions and hold different beliefs. One thing that is important to understand is that it may not be easy to determine what any religion has contributed to civilization but it has for sure resulted in the death and suffering of millions of people. To be clear I am not talking about spirituality here, because a truly spiritual person only has one religion i.e. serving those who are suffering and ill. Holy and unholy, religious and irreligious may sound like similar words but that isn't true. Religion binds you in beliefs, faith, and in a certain lifestyle, where you may not even have the freedom to wear clothes of your choice, even those that are governed by your religion. In short, you have to live your life according to your religion if you truly follow it. However, spirituality gives you true freedom.

It doesn't matter which religion you are attached to but you will notice that of all the spiritual people that have walked this earth, none have ever lived their life according to the sayings of the religious scripts but instead according to their wise perspectives. I am not sure if they have prayed and served the God they believed in but I am very sure that all of them have served and helped people who are ill or suffering, One thing is clear this, that all the people who have suffered or have been hurt, due to terrorism or due to protest against some religious group, have for sure seen dead people. Because a living person will never do the disgusting task of putting a sword to the throats of innocent masses in the name of religion.

Such a person has been killed by his society, his religion, his nation and he has been betrayed even by his own parents, his friends, and relatives. Together all of them have attacked and destroyed his power to think, his perspective, and his belief system. And like filling gunpowder in an empty cylinder they have filled his body with hate in the name of religion, history, and beliefs. This is the reality of every person who has picked up a gun in the name of religion and is fighting senseless wars, killing innocent people with whom he has nothing to do with.

2. A situation of instability

Our life always seems unstable to us. However, our wish is always the opposite of this, that everything should be in our control. We all want such a degree of control that not even a leaf should fall if we don't want it to. And the funny thing is that this is possible as well. But to understand that we first have to understand what we are capable of, what level of control we have over ourselves. Nature shares her power only with those who have the patience to use it well. This is an extremely serious branch of science and as we traverse down deeper in it we will find ourselves moving closer and closer to the point from where this universe started. We will talk seriously about this topic but for the time being, let's try to understand an unstable man and the inconvenience he creates.

In news often we see about a variety of crimes being committed and we don't want that any crime to be committed in this world or rather no crime should be committed in our world but the reality is that we commit many crimes whether knowingly or unknowingly and most of us often ignore the chaos which has been caused in this world due to those acts of ours.

And all these crimes share a common reason i.e. the unstable circumstances of life. For example, if you are a bit rich then you probably have some maids and servants to do your work for you. Have you noticed that if you double the salary you give to your servants today then it won't affect your financial condition? You won't lose much but your maid's life will improve exponentially. Their children will get better futures and their life will have more happiness in them, and they will probably feel that life indeed is a gift and an opportunity. The truth is that knowingly or unknowingly we have made many people feel awful, taking the joy and resources or opportunities away from those who had the true right to it. What can be a bigger crime than the fact that because of you the wishes of someone's children were left unfulfilled, and this harsh fact remains in their young mind that because of the small paycheck of their father they can't ask for toys. What can be more unfortunate than this? And what is the reason for this greedy behavior? Only that our greed has become uncontrollable?

This reality might seem weird but we have to accept that the reason for every poor family is that a rich family couldn't control their greed. Even a blind person could see that there is enough land in our world that every family can have a home and there is enough food that no one should have to sleep with an empty stomach. But when even with enough resources such situations arise that some people have everything and some people have nothing then the first reason that comes to mind is that greed in humans has crossed all limits. Although there is a difference that the circumstances of someone being rich or poor are very complex and everyone faces the possibility of being either in their life. Some succeed and some don't and the reason behind that is part of a different aspect of science which we will discuss later. But when a successful and wealthy person ignores his responsibilities towards society then we can understand the reason behind this by considering their unstable mental condition. The unfortunate thing is that it seems like everyone today is of an unstable mental condition. Some are too worried about earning money and some are too worried about what they have lost. And some are so mentally unstable that they aren't afraid to kill or even die.

3. Human society and wealth

Our civilization shares an ancient relationship with wealth. When humans were primates and the modern comforts of today's world did not exist, even in those primitive times, wealth took the form of livestock (animals), food, and habitable caves and shelters. Anyone who had the access to all such comforts was called the 'Leader' or considered a powerful man. This was a common situation however in modern times the circumstances have taken a turn. Money has become the reason for life between birth and death. There was a time when a person's physical capabilities were of the essence. The healthier a person was physical, the more work they could do and any person could earn their living just by doing physical labor. However, in the modern world, such a mind-blowing system has been developed which rewards nothing to the people working the hardest but anyone sitting in the first-class office sipping on the comforts of life can earn enough money to fulfill all their desires without lifting a finger. The rich are getting richer while the poor working relentlessly barely earn enough to make ends meet. And the result of this is that a big part of the world is living in absence of the necessities of life and contrastingly a small part of the world is living their life as if this world was made to entertain only them. In such circumstances, it seems that the world and everything in it was made for the pleasure of the strongest people.

Certainly, such a system could prove destructive for any developed civilization. And can a society, where such circumstances and suffering prevails, even be called a developed civilization?

The matter of concern however is the matter that in a world where man has gone so far as to be unfazed by the fact that for their supposed 'comforts' such as the meat on their table some innocent life had to suffer a painful fate. Can such a man even bat an eye towards the homeless and starving men sleeping on the cold pavement in the shadow of his cozy manor?

Such a situation cannot be blamed on a single problem but the reality is that the qualities of humanity that distinguish humans from animals have perished and all that is left is the carcasses of human beings with the base animal instincts – ready to kill their fellow beings for their comfort and survival.

The concept of money was brought up to assist in the exchange of commodities and to replace the barter system prevalent at the time. The system of exchanging money for things you need, corrupted by greed, has been converted into a mad race for getting more and more money fueled by the outrageous dreams of some monstrous people to own the world. Life's success is measured in money and the aim is to get as much money as you can whether by hook or by crook. Granted some people have the necessary wit and brains to exploit people and make money but still prefer to remain far from it. But the fact remains that faced with the corrupted concept of money, no matter how it was corrupted, the world would've been a better place with no money at all.

4. Man and Science:

When we talk about science then we are driving the conversation in the right direction. This is because science has solved the problems of humanity and led us to the in more off whereas more civilized and comfortable life. In my opinion, a scientist is an artist in the true sense of the term. Religion has not given much to science but science has given everything. We should be thankful to the people who walk the difficult path of science and truth. They dare to look at the world with all its wonder and accept its complexity and secrets.

Today our life is so dependent on machines that we can't imagine a functioning human society in the absence of these gifts of science. The reality is that in the modern world the average man knows more about this world than the smartest bunch of people who walked the earth a few thousand years ago. If you think about the comforts you are used to you will come to understand how wondrous it is if we view it from the perspective of the earlier civilizations. We have cars, electricity, mobile phones, ACs in the summers, and heaters in the winter. All of these are given to us by the evolution of science. But among all the wonders and boons of science, unfortunately, it also resulted in the development of a system where all these amazing inventions are only available to the rich.

We will try our best to understand these differences but first, we should express our sincere thankfulness to the inventors of gadgets like diesel engines, electricity, mobile phones, etc. These gadgets and their applications have become inherent to our way of life. These inventions are so revolutionary that the common man can't imagine a world without them. We should be indebted to the people who have made such gadgets and to those who continue to spend their lives developing and inventing things to make this world a better place.

There hasn't been one aspect that was meant to harm society however some foul-minded and corrupted humans used science to create destructive tools which can probably end the world at any time. Looking at history we can understand that every war initiated by mankind was due to their futile anger and ego resulting in using the destructive abilities of science. This is the wrong use of science and science should only be used to fuel the progress of mankind. And along with this the comfort brought by the various inventions of science belong to everyone and should be made available to every person. Money shouldn't be the deciding factor upon which the quality of life of people is decided.

Chapter 5

The universe and the animal kingdom

1. The beginning of the universe

Anything begins with the creation of it. Whenever the creator creates something it has a specific purpose to serve. The universe is the one in which we live, earth and our homes are merely forms of it. In reality, we are parts of this universe, the existence of which is full of secrets and is full of immense energy. It is never-ending and indestructible.

What is the purpose of the creation of our universe and why did conscious life only develop on earth and not other planets, and is this life part of a grand scheme of things? The answer to these questions and more can only be found if we look deeply at the process of creation of this universe and the secrets hidden among the energies of this world. And if we can understand the energy behind the creation of the world we will certainly be able to find an answer to many other existential problems and figure out our place in this universe.

When unbounded energy is focused at one point then that energy takes the form of matter and when that matter disperses it takes the form of energy again. This peculiar nature of matter may seem imaginative to some but this is the true form of it. According to scientists, this universe is slowly expanding but the fact that something which is already limitless is expanding isn't a concerning matter. But the matter that does concern us is that in this never-ending universe, how far does our existence go and what role are we supposed to fulfill, and if we are insignificant to the purpose of the universe then why is it that we still survive.

This universe is made up of 3 things: Matter, Place, and Time. We can't say that science doesn't know much about the matter. We know about the creation and nature of atoms and other smaller parts of matter. The 2 things leftovers are Place and time. Both are of such nature that they can't be understood by way of experiments alone. Which is the reason why many secrets are still left to be uncovered hidden in these dimensions.

When we talk about space or place then we talk about the vessel in which we are present or the thing in association with which time finds its meaning. Space works on the same rules for something as huge as the sun or as small as an atom. In reality, space is imaginative, it isn't real but we can sense it and see it.

To understand this with an example, if we let a common man's life be of 100 years, then in this life that man sees a lot of days and experiences a lot of things. But in the end, he dies and returns to an abyss of darkness. If you close your eyes for a minute you only see darkness however when you open them you see the wonderful world around you. So in what is existence – Is it the abyss of darkness in front of you when you close your eyes or the colorful world you see around you when you open your eyes. In reality, existence is the abyss of darkness we see with our eyes closed because that abyss cannot be destroyed. You have to understand that you aren't seeing it with your eyes, it is already there, you only notice it now. After a while, after you have perished and the world comes to an end too you will see this darkness again only this time with open eyes. Thus we have to realize that the endless abyss of darkness is the reality and truth of creation, not the perishable state of existence as we see it now - i.e. the world, life, and space.

All of this is an illusion that has been made by time and in the end, it will all be taken over by time itself. To put this into simple words, whatever we experience in our life is because of the compulsion of the vulnerability and qualities of the material and energy we are made up of. Under such circumstances, we are forced to buy into the illusion of time and space even though we are wise about its reality. Like we have to live here forever.

Till now, all the genius minds of the world from Albert Einstein to Stephen Hawkings have discussed and presented a varying range of views and theories about the creation of this universe, but there is still much confusion among the scholars as to which theory is a sure shot solution to the question of the creation of the universe. There is still no specific answer to how, where, and when the universe started. Even a bigger question yet is - Why did conscious life take form only on planet Earth, and from that life why did only homosapiens advance or evolve as far as they did such that today when we say 'Life on Earth' it is synonymous with 'Humans on Earth'. Science has no answer to these questions and they are still among the many secrets of this world. India's famous mountain range, the Himalayas, is home to people who can be called 'Super humans'. They don't belong to any specific religion and neither is there a need to look at them from a religious perspective. When some people and scholars got into touch with these superhumans over time and asked them about the universe, the only answer they got was that God wants some things to stay secret. What is necessary has already been revealed to humankind.

Our knowledge of this universe is certainly very limited and primitive. Because if this wasn't the case after achieving such a level of growth and sophistication in society, there wouldn't still be such petty differences and imbalance in life that on one side people are dying from eating too much and on the other hand there are millions dying of starvation.

2. Chances of Life in the Universe

Before searching for the chances of life it is important that we properly understand the meaning of life. In our day-to-day life, we may forget that we are a bunch of chemicals.

This is a different matter that the matter of birth and death is one that even science doesn't understand.

To understand the creation and secrets of life on earth, many experiments were taken up but none was successful enough to convincingly lay out the answers. But we can say that there are chances of life on all planets in the universe where sources of water and energy are present. It is important to understand that without enough heat and light from the sun life cannot exist either. There are a lot of vital sources of energy but the Sun is the most vital and efficient source of energy.

The universe supports endless possibilities of life considering its size. But the major problem is that the distance between galaxies is humongous, and even for highly developed species, it would be very difficult and almost impossible to develop the necessary technology to traverse this huge space. It would be surprising to know that time and time again scientists have found various radio waves and signals that could've been emitted only by a developed life form. But unfortunately, all such signals have been so far away from us that even if we were able to travel at the speed of light it would take us 2 to 3 hundred years to reach them. And even if we were able to go there considering that it took about the same or more time for these signals to reach us, it would be very likely that there would be nothing left of them now. This does put into perspective however how large this world is.

How life developed on Earth, explains one thing life has great power in it and this power is capable of surviving even the harshest of conditions, whether it be hunger, thirst, hot or cold, illness, or other kinds of mortal struggles, life finds a way through all this and moves forward through everything. If we look at history then we find that in the past of the earth many such events have taken place which should've resulted at the end of all life on it. But even if an entire species was wiped out then another evolved into existence, with all the required qualities to survive in the new environment. From different body types to the food chain, everything evolves and changes according to the changes in the environment. This isn't a common thing to happen, it is indeed a wondrous quality that has provided living creatures the ability to evolve and develop further. And seeing this quality it would be appropriate to say that life must exist in some form or the other in every corner of this universe. Whether the creatures are similar to human beings or something else, life is for sure present in all corners of the universe.

Chapter 6

The secret to success and prosperity

In today's world science is capable enough that it is possible that not just every human but even every animal can lead a happy and prosperous life, however, still there is a sort of instability spread everywhere around the world. Some People have nothing and some people have too much. Some struggle to even get drinking water and some have Olympian swimming pools in their backyards. When we look at such massive inequality in society, the mind does wonder about which power is it that decides who becomes rich and who becomes poor. What are the special qualities in the rich and what are the problems in the poor that result in such massive differences in their life even though essentially they are the same and belong to the same species i.e. they are both humans?

This isn't the case that poor people don't work hard enough or that the rich work harder than the poor. The reality is that a poor person works for 10 hours a day and a rich person only works 5 hours i.e. half of the work the poor person does. But even with hard work, the amount a common man earns in a month can be earned by a millionaire in merely a day. There can be many reasons for this and various experts of finance will give their different opinions. But in reality, the solution to this has never been found by anyone yet.

Because if a solution was found then today the standard of living of common people like you and me would be the same as the standard of living for the president of the USA. And maybe someday when the solution to this problem is found the world will have neither the poor nor the billionaires.

This is indeed a very interesting game. And the reason why it is so interesting is that there is no telling when a new player can take the game in their favor with a new trick. The game of Success and prosperity is like that of the game of chess, it has no end and neither does someone's win over these last too long. If you look at the world deeply, you will notice that many people in the world were born into poor households but used their superior intellect to find such loopholes in the system, based on which they pulled off such huge scams that they are even difficult to imagine. Technically these people are criminals and scammers but the only chance for affecting change lies hidden in protest. Instead of protesting the circumstances if you keep accepting them then the chances of achieving success in life will die off with the act of acceptance. These scammers are the kind of people who protested against the system and as a result, were successful in making the things they wanted in their life come true. However, the path chosen by these people was wrong and now they are facing the consequences.

From my perspective, a successful person can align his well-being with the well-being of others and not one who wants to benefit himself at the cost of others.

Success like this is never stable and in the end, its results are always destructive. However, on the other hand, achieving success is morally blue and long-lasting. But achieving success morally is only possible when you are willing to contribute something to society and human civilization. This contribution can be in any form, whether it be an invention, a work of art, aching, or a solution. Always think deeply about what you are contributing to society, as a result of which I can gain all those things from the society which I need. On the road to success, this is the biggest success for any person.

The secret to success and wealth is immensely complex and mysterious. It has many aspects, from human psychology to luck and hard work, it is a mixture of a lot of things. One by one we will try to understand all the aspects of it:-

1. What is called success?

Most people think that having money is called a success, which according to me is a huge mistake. A person with such a mindset faces a lot of problems on the path to success and even after all the hardships there is no guarantee to them achieving success.

The meaning of success is such an ability to do a task or such a technique to doing a task that the things you can do easily start seeming impossible to a common man. In reality, it is not guaranteed that every time you can do something new and amazing every time but if you can do what you do with such talent and dedication that no one can do it better than you, then that is success in itself. The ability to convert this talent and dedication into a way of earning money is the next step but the first thing is to be sure that you are completely capable of doing what you do.

Most people only think about getting money by any means and due to this try all the wrong ways. Due to the absence of enough information, they achieve nothing and instead face losses. Some even degenerate so much so that they choose to murder and hooliganism, some still get some money by such questionable means while others get nothing still.

This is a very common saying that good deeds result in good results and bad deeds result in bad results but even so people go down the wrong way and do bad deeds, this is a concerning matter. Such people are very selfish and have petty ambitions, don't believe in anything like their responsibilities to society, and don't think twice about hurting others a lot even if they benefit only a little from it. When such people can earn money then the people of a certain group start believing that even by choosing the wrong path and doing the wrong deeds it is possible to earn success and wealth. Such people can see the glory and the money but the dangers and the losses that they have to face along the path go unseen by them, and due to this ignorance most of them end up losing their life.

I accept that money is everything in life but I would like to remind you that we get this life only once and we should never have the audacity to play around with it. Try every possible way to achieve success but not ones that take away the rights of others. Immoral acts bring with them innumerable problems.

This much should be well understood that the true meaning of success is doing your tasks properly and the ability to face the problems in your life. If you can do this much then you should assume that more than half of the work is already done. After this, the second aspect is the redressal of myths. Most people live their life believing myths and not accepting reality even though they know the truth. Every person should accept this one thing that in this world your biggest supporter is you, how can someone else find the solutions for you. This life is yours and you have to investigate every aspect of it yourself and when you go out to find the solution then automatically such opportunities will present themselves to you which you can't even imagine. After All, this time is yours and you are free to make your choice as to what you want to do. All you need is the right understanding of what is right and what is wrong. Searching for life's meaning and its immortal truth is another matter which is far too complex for a normal person to understand. But nothing is impossible, many secrets of this world have been revealed for everyone, this is a different concern that those people who couldn't find the path to even unstable wealth, can't even be expected to find a way to stable and everlasting wealth.

If we move away from this topic and towards a new aspect, then we will be able to understand another meaning of success, which is self-satisfaction. However there is one important thing to remember about self-satisfaction, this word is only for those people who are in the end stage of their life. Such people should surely accept what they have and move towards death with ease of mind. But those who are young, with a few kids in the house, should stay away from self-satisfaction. Because this distances you from worldly attachments. They should make sure that what they have is enough so that their acts don't push their family into suffering and poverty.

Usually, we get to see such examples where people don't even have enough to eat but still, they pretend as if they are living the most comfortable life. In reality, such people only do such things to hide their failures and problems in life. Thus to make success possible in life you must estimate your capabilities and move forward in life, not only for yourself but for your society as well, and you will achieve success for sure.

2. Important rules to achieve success:-

When you compete to get something then a huge struggle is bound to happen. And the struggle is such that no one fights anyone visibly but using the problems and abilities of the system everyone tries to take their part of the pie. The problem is that no one has a fixed limit due to which some people go much farther than the rest and some people are left behind. And still, some people become so savage that they get ready to kill or even die in front of the world when they see something that could benefit them, this is something no one can disagree with.

This war for resources is between humans and every animal on this earth, however, animals only want enough to satisfy their basic needs, they don't plan for the future or gather and hoard resources for future generations. And humans are so greedy for their own and future needs that they don't mind leaving someone else to starve if it means they are getting something.

In this war who will win and who will lose depends on some basic things. If a man keeps these things in mind his victory is almost certain

A) Resolution

To complete any task you need to have a solid resolution. For people who have an unstable mind and change their decisions, again and again, the chances of people achieving success are doubtful. Make sure that you solidify this in your mind that you can achieve your dreams and you can achieve success before time runs out and take more than what is destined for you. You may not believe in God but you should never stop believing in your power and its presence.

If you look at history then you can see clearly that those who had great resolutions, stuck to their word and the world bowed in front of them. However, it is seen many times that even people with great resolutions don't reach a level or stature of importance. But there is no need to be discouraged from this because when you aim at ruling the entire world, I will tell you in clear words, that such ambitions will never succeed. For example consider the many militants and terrorists of the world, all of them set out to rule the world but today there is no trace left of them.

Thus one more important thing to understand is that it might be possible to win this world with kindness but not with force and arrogance. In reality when the resolution is based on the eternal truth, then it will for sure be fulfilled. But if someone wishes that others should be hurt then they will have to face a fierce protest. And protest can be faced to a certain level but after that level defeat is certain.

The second magical change of resolution that you will notice in your life will be internal guidance. When your wishes are true and moral then you struggle against the world with all your power to achieve them, then you will notice that there is a feeling inside you which tells you where to go and what to do, due to which you will find yourself even doing the impossible. This feeling is your self-confidence towards the truth and such confidence can only arise in those who stay true to their resolution.

If we go even deeper then we will find many more aspects of the resolution. But who can make resolutions and who can stay true to their resolutions, this is also an interesting matter. Usually, people have dreams like that of the Sheikh Chilli or in simpler words, some people are like Sheikh Chilli that they dream of being a millionaire at night and form strategies to achieve that and when they wake up in the morning they forget what they had even thought about at night.

Their dreams are so big that they become millionaires in dreams, make plans for the morning but forget about when they wake up. People like this can not even do business or jobs, having a resolution is far for them. In today's world more than most people's situation is like this only.

To make ourselves understand that this thing is making a barrier in our way is important. This thing can only be understood by self-introspection because till the time we will not clean ourselves from inside there will be no space for good. We should accept that Success is only for good people.

I accept the goons, thieves, earn money too and the reality is also that they are holding big posts in politics. They have some reasons that we will clarify. But morality has its power and the development of these qualities does not provide benefits is not possible but we must stay on our wishes and resolutions.

B. Hard Work

Hard work is a word that is not digested by the most ambitious people. Most people start searching for shortcuts when they hear about the hard work. Or most people see that hard work is not required in achievements, we should use our brains instead. To some extent these things are right, but without hard work and practice you expect to get succeeded in life then there are minimal chances of it. A successful person cannot deny the fact that to work hard in fact about hard work one should assure the difference between hard work and donkey labor. I will never support donkey labor because if only by laboring or wages one could be able to achieve everything then the world's factory workers and laborers were the richest. Most people think physical work is only hard work and physical work is very tiring so most people avoid doing it but this is a wrong definition. If we define hard work with the right point of view then its definition could be

That we should do our work that gives the best results in the end. Now if there come great hardships in the way one should solve it who do hard work. Physical work is also a part of it but hard work will only be meaningful and effective when it will get a correct direction. Most people do not complete one work and switch to another. In this situation, even one work does not get completed and we get failure instead. If we do an inspection we will see that the richest businessmen are beggars now. These people for the sake of their talents of solving the problems and resolutions reached certain heights in their careers but for investing in one after another project they got ruined. They did do a lot of hard work but if this hard work got a central point the results could be better. They could not even understand that some work can give meaningful results when the world is in such a great need for it, important creations always give harm.

In our lives, we make certain decisions that we have to make ourselves, for all the work and advice we cannot depend on anyone for every time. Hard Work is like that only. In our regular life, we should do an inspection of where our life is going, in which direction, or we should try to see where our hard work is paying to a meaningful outcome and it is transformative.

If we look at the regular lives of some people we will see that they are moving in a direction of economic hard work only. From day to night their aim is similar and they spend their life like this only. When they are advised or asked to take a different step in a different direction they get stressed as if they have a huge problem. In this case, even after so much hard work, there is no chance of success in their lives.

Hard Work only results in meaningful results when there is room for changes and opportunities in life and we can assure it by taking every opportunity in our way.

C. Positive Thinking

This earth's headdress is difficult to understand. On one side a man puts all of their heart and soul into normal achievement, on another side, in some billionaire's home when a child is born he gets a life that a normal person can only imagine.

There is no requirement of getting scared of this reality accepting this reality with understanding that we have all the possibilities present. Most people don't concentrate on the avenues available to them, they think that we can never do this work or we don't have this or that things to do this work, they search for these kinds of excuses.

To take out from this hate and complete the work with each impossibility and think out the ways to make it possible is the most important aspect. Don't forget that there is a war going on in this world, a little bit of omission causes huge damage in no time.

The stillness of mind is important for a person who wishes for the level which is not the fate for normal people. Rising above all with something special is only possible when some different and important activities are performed and this is possible when our thinking is positive. In daily lives, contexts like this are made. There are distractions, at least in the lives of businessmen. Contexts like these are present so situations like this can only be confronted when our mind is at peace and there is stillness of mind.

Positive thinking is not only important to get success in life, positive thinking is also so that we can have the remembrance that we are humans and how we should live our lives. With our daily routines and problems, most people are weeping their lives behind this. Having a negative look out towards the situation is a big reason. We have to accept that we have not created this world so providing a solution to each problem of this world is not our thing.

D. Proper Management Of Money:-

No matter how rich a person is he should understand where he has to put a stop to his expenses. Leaving eight to ten people of this world all others come in this category only. There is nothing like people are unable to earn, they earn but they celebrate their small success with loud celebrations that coming situations get wasted before. If we search then there is a huge list of the millionaires present who were rich and sometimes have big names but where are they in this world nobody knows! If we move without any adjustment being created between income and expenses then the best person cannot rise from a certain level.

Today, the world's rich are getting richer and the poor are getting poorer. The basic reason behind this is not that poor people are wasteful or they don't have the mind but the main reason is that poor people are unable to save more than a certain level of their income. His earnings are limited for his family's survival and no huge investment in the capital also cannot be done. With which no new way of income

Can be opened. Apart from this, rich people have a huge income so they invest in the market on the things that are important for daily life. Because of fixed requirements, their business runs well and they get rich by day-night speed.

This art can also be called the right management of money and this possibility is present with every person. The only small requirement is to seek nearby presented avenues. The calculation of how much money we have and how it can be invested so that the better to best outcomes can be inhaled.

Big companies and industrial units earn millions-billions of money every year. Their businesses run well while we see from the general point of view, it is so difficult for the vegetable vendor to get a customer. So how can these companies earn so much money that after committing every expense the owner is left with so much unimagined money every year? The main reason for this is the right arrangement of money however there are investments from the bank in these businesses and most types of scams. But if common people do scams and get the arrangement of money then

Because getting money by scamming people is also a very difficult task. Because if everyone was capable of getting money by scamming people then no one would choose to be a laborer and everyone would have been rich. However I don't support any immoral task, but in reality it is impossible to find a solution for it without accepting it.

Money is such a thing that it is required for your every need. And it is not possible that you get money from everywhere. To get something from society you have to contribute something as well. The only ailment that can give you everything without you having to give anything is called being rich. If we look at it properly we will see these basic reasons why a small group of people are running a vast empire due to some special reasons. The history behind this is extensive and in the end the conversation stops at the great inventions due to which today we have things like mobile phones, cars, airplanes and electricity. The debt of these gadgets can never be fully paid by the human civilization, but there usage in the path of success has resulted in a small group of people having immense power, due to which the human society got divided into sections i.e. the rich and the poor. For a developed civilization, nothing can be more unfortunate than this that on one hand there is food rotting and on the other hand people are dying of starvation.

Expectations can only be kept from those people who not only understand the system and try to move forward but also have a kind behavior and make efforts to help others move forward as well. Because as important as it is to use a guidebook wisely, more important is that the guide is present first.

Chapter 7

The powers running the universe

Science today has become very successful and it is moving towards many amazing inventions in the future. But from a realistic point of view, the truth is that we know basically nothing. Whenever we look at the problems related to the human civilization or the animal kingdom and we think about finding a solutions to these problems then usually we find ourselves pondering about more than just the earth, and we have to find the answer to the questions of who made this universe and which power is it that is regulating all the events and changes taking place in the universe right now. Scientists know how the sun works but no one knows how big the universe is. There are many theories about how it came into existence and the most famous one is that of the Big Bang by Stephen Hawking, which states that this universe came into being with a huge explosion. The simple meaning of this theory is that matter can be understood as energy and energy can be understood as matter. In a scientific point of view all these theories can be understood and accepted to a certain extent but for the people who are trying to find the truth all these theories are completely baseless.

1. Gravity

Sir Issac Newton was the first person whose brain questioned why everything falls downwards not upwards. Thanks to his curiosity and efforts, we now know that a power like Gravity is present in this universe, which is omnipresent and keeps everything attached to the surface of the earth.

Gravity plays a very important role in the existence of the universe, from the revolution of planets to the creation of humongous stars, a lot of it goes to gravity. But in reality what is gravity, why are two molecules attracted towards each other. This series of questions stops at the point where no one even understands what is happening and why it is happening. The biggest reason for this is that humans can investigate the molecules of visible matter but not the things they can't see. There is a limit to the level of microscopic things scientists can investigate but after that even they can't see anything but darkness. Thus the reality is that truly everything is nothing i.e. everything is 0.

It is very mysterious that even though gravity is invisible, it still plays such a big role in the universe.

Every molecule of this world is pulling another molecule towards it, in simple words it is very chaotic. There is a lot of instability here, or in even simpler words, prisoners have broken out of the jail and created chaos in the entire city. A major reason for problems and suffering in our society is that the development and creation of animal life on eartwereas not required.

It's not just about animal civilization but the entire universe is an inessential development. It is a result of one instability or mistake. And maybe when all the molecules are successful in being joined to each other then maybe this mistake will be rectified and this mystery will be solved. And again there will be peace and quiet for a very long time.

Although gravity is a common force, the amount of chaos caused by it is not caused by any other force in the Universe. Its most mysterious creation are the various stars in the galaxy

Our sun is not ours alone, but the millions and billions of stars visible in the night sky, all exist due to gravity. Gravity is the main force due to which the nucleus accumbens progress begins in the star and it can cut through even the deepest darkest parts of the galaxy and shine brightly, and its light can ignite life into everything around it and forces it to change. And if circumstances are favorable then some magical things can take place like the ones that happened on Earth.

This process is similar in the entire universe and there is no doubt that life is infinite, it is spread all across the universe. But its huge and unparalleled size is a limitation for all developed civilizations. It is impossible to traverse the boundaries set by the universe and maybe it's creating forces did it because no developed civilization could attack an under developed civilization to take over its resources and rights. Why wonder about anywhere else, we can see these things on Earth as well. Everyone knows how for their insatiable hunger, humans have misused and exploited all the animals on Earth and their rights.

There is a very famous Hollywood movie 'Avatar', it is just a work of fiction but we can see how if man was given a chance to go to another planet then how far humans will be willing to hurt and exploit other lifeforms just for a little benefit and resources.

Keeping all this in mind we can say that Gravity is that essential force of this universe that decides both its creation and its conclusion. Science knows a lot about this force but not enough to make airplanes which can be free from the effects of gravity and can fly easily. Until such inventions take place, petrol is the only way it seems.

2. Space:

The most mind-boggling aspect of our universe is its size. Whether we consider the sun or moon or the entire galaxy, everything is spread across a vast space but in comparison to this the size and span of the universe is so huge that it can only be understood a bit by physicists, the rest can't even imagine.

The first requirement for the existence of anything is choosing a place according to the shape and type of the item. From this basic logic, it can be learned that the first thing that would have come into existence in this universe would have been space. But what is space? This can be understood with the help of an example. How far can a fish swim inside an ocean, it can swim as far and wide as the ocean i.e. wherever there is water. If the ocean were to slowly freeze over then according to the shrinking size of the water the space where the fish can swim will also shrink accordingly. In reality, the span of space defines the qualities and tasks of the things within. Time also plays an essential role in this. But time doesn't stop any object from moving in the universe, instead of like the ocean freezing over time, it also stops itself from moving to stop objects from moving. This means that if something in our universe crosses a certain limit and moves as fast or perhaps faster than light, then even if it traveled for a thousand years it will find itself stuck in the same place from where it went at lightspeed. Because compared to the speed of the object, the speed of time was less. However the object would be able to time travel like this, i.e. it will be able to survive for a very long time, outside the constraints of time.

This is a very weird and mysterious topic but the relationship of space and time is just like this. Space is also what we see every night and space is also where electrons revolve around the atom's nucleus in set paths. The space within an atom is much more interesting and mysterious than even the space we can see with our eyes. Because here the systems of time and gravity cannot work. At this level we get to know a different face of science. Where it is difficult for even scientists to figure out the reason behind various events or the forces at play. The biggest problem with an atom is its microscopic size. And to think that this microscopic matter is the basis for the entire universe. From this one thing is clear that when we move from the huge planets to the microscopic atoms, the physics doesn't stay the same. And when unlimited speed is also an aspect then time also shows new characteristics.

Chapter 8

Become human before becoming rich

You can find a million benefits of being rich and can dream as many dreams of it as you want and you may even become a billionaire but you can't change one eternal truth. In this world, even the greatest people cannot guarantee that something will happen, but death is something that comes with a 100 percent guarantee. You cannot deny the truth regarding death and the worst aspect of death for any man is that they can't take anything with them.

If you look at it deeply then most of the people in the world who are very rich, only start giving away to charity or become interested in social work, only after becoming older than 60. A big reason for this is that after a certain age their ability to feel and enjoy things start fading away and their body stops working as well as they want it to. Only then do they realize the truth, a truth they have to accept even if they don't want to. Because as everyone knows, Death is certain, but how many people do you know who plan and live their life with this fact in mind? Almost no one does this. But after getting older than 60, you can see death coming towards you clearly and no matter how much money you have you can't stop it.

1. Estimate your capabilities:-

In their usual life due to a bad perspective most people live a very bad life. Even though they have the capability to live a better and amazing life. And if we look deeply then we realize that it's not just that we can improve our own life but we can do things for others which can make us feel like our life is successful.

When I say successful life I don't mean that you are out partying in bars late at night or going on a cruise on a yacht. All these things are for the ghosts, not the living. Only the ghosts roam around the streets at 1 or 2 in the night, not the living. Thus the first thing you have to ensure is that you are taking steps towards a better life not towards a life of ghosts. If you look carefully then you will realize that billionaires and their children keep traveling around the world, from one hotel to another or from one beach to another. But why, the ocean is the same everywhere and hotels are barely any fun, you can sleep in the bed or eat in the café but that's about it, it's the same everywhere.

It isn't possible that you get to eat silver someplace and think let's go there, we will get to eat gold, let's taste it. What is the point of going so many places after all, what is the special thing you are looking for? Can this roaming around all the time ever beat the peace and quiet of staying at one point. This constant roaming around of the rich can only be explained by how when you let a dog have a bone, then the dog will start biting and licking the bone so hard that his teeth will start bleeding but the dog will think that the blood is coming out of the bone and it will bite even harder. In the end the result would be that all of the dog's teeth will fall out and by the time it will realize, it would have been too late.

Thus we should make sure that before becoming rich we try becoming a better human being, or else the money might make us a ghost or dog.

It is possible to take any task to fruition when such a person is behind such a task who before taking the next step forward always considers if there is a possibility of going further or not.

And this kind of behavior cannot be expected from those who consider partying and traveling as success. To develop and use this quality is only possible if you properly estimate your own capabilities.

Get rid of the fear inside of you, it doesn't matter who you might be afraid of losing or how much power or money you are afraid of losing. It is possible that you will have to bear some losses, if you are afraid of losing everything then consider this, you didn't bring anything with you when you came into this world, then it makes no sense of being afraid to lose. You should always keep in mind that you shouldn't ever get so involved in the game that knowingly or unknowingly your acts bring tears to someone's eyes or wipe the smile off of someone's face.

2. Recognize yourself:

Usually when you see two people fighting then you can often hear someone saying " You don't know who I am", but the matter of fact is that, how many people are there who even know who they themselves really are. Whenever you get a chance to sit in a quiet place alone you should think about who you really are. If you change your definition and remove things like your name, your relationships, your place etc and consider your existence in the context of the entire universe and ask yourself who you are then you will realize that almost half of our life's problems will disappear.

Humans are amazing dream watchers and I believe that even animals must have dreams in deep sleep, but unfortunately they can't really tell anyone about it. But unlike animals humans get sad when they start to imagine things. Imagination is a good thing, I actually believe that imagination is a gateway to reality, if you know how to open it ,that is. And unfortunately 99 percent of the people can't make their imaginations reality, even though they live in their imaginary world most of the time. In this situation every second there is a big clash between the real world and the imaginary, and as a result thoughts of helplessness, hopelessness and even suicide take control of the mind of that person.

If you free yourself from the imaginary world and look at the real world and think deeply upon who you really are then you will realize the truth that you aren't here for all eternity. We have some time here and after that is finished, we will have to go from here.

This seems like common knowledge because everyone knows that everyone will have to die. But not many people live with this feeling of mortality or acceptance of death in their life. The biggest difference between a smart and a stupid person is that the smart people accept it and the stupid people deny it. All the dictators that have existed in the world, all were very stupid. They always wanted to achieve something that didn't exist. As a result all of them died a horrible death and in the process millions died an untimely death because of them.

A knowledgeable person who has a tendency to accept things, lives in reality. There are several identifiers of such people. The first indicator is that such people like to live a simple life. But these people have immense talent and they complete whatever task they undertake, they are people of such an immense presence that they can find gold wherever they dig. Completing any task is an art and this art isn't known better by anyone but these people.

The second important indicator that we can notice in those who live life by the truth is that such people always tend to be ready to help others. Whether it takes money, power or any other kind of help these people are always ready. And if the circumstances ask, these people will be willing to face a loss themselves to protect others from it.

Seeing the present conditions of the world, our world really needs such people. Everyone is set on taking everything, it doesn't matter who it belongs to. "If someone's children are dying of hunger, then it's not like I can do anything about it, I'll buy the newest Mercedes though". The constantly deteriorating mindset of people is going to result in some very savage and horrible things to happen in the future. If you want to see how far people can go to prove themselves different and special from others, then you should go ask the masons, bricklayers of the monumental skyscrapers and laborers how much they were paid. Or you will realize how much the 'saviors' or doctors get paid when you have to do rounds of the hospital going here and there to get yourself treated.

In my opinion such people aren't truly alive, in reality they are half dead corpses. Because you can't expect such cold and savage behavior from a living person. Today every such person who is willing to do anything for money is basically dead and he was murdered by our society and our capitalist perspective. Such people only learned one thing from their childhood that more money means you will be able to get more happiness in life. And taking this teaching as an excuse everyone sets out to make their world better even if it means destroying someone else's.

If you really want to know yourself then you have to rise above a certain level of thinking. From the day you start worrying about others and are able to connect with the feelings and emotions of other people then you will feel as if the world was made for you and this world needs you. When you start understanding yourself and are able to figure out the goal which you think you were given life for or a goal which you think is worth giving your life to, then it becomes easier to live through the phases of life when you have no one to stand by you. At least this is what my experience says.

3. Learn how to make decisions

Sometimes situations turn out to be so bad that even a smart man's mind stops working. This is a very common thing because when we do not know something like this will happen, how can we predict what is going to happen next. When we are unaware of what is going to happen next then it is usual for even a smart man to get confused.

I remember when I was young, a program was telecasted on the discovery channel in which Oprah Winfrey was talking to a famous Indian writer. That writer said something to Oprah that I remember to this day: your future depends on your situations and it depends on you how you tackle your situations.

Most of the people are of fateful thinking, for them, there is no better answer than this. In totality, the truth that comes in front of us is that when a person becomes weak with his self-confidence, the situation of confusion arises and it becomes difficult for a person to take decisions even for petty things and to decide what to do and what not to.

If we look closely, we will find that people who don't put any thought and get going on any path, become more successful instead of those who calculate land to the sky for small things. There is a very famous Hollywood movie "Van Helsing" in which the heroine was named "Anna".in that film, the heroine faces a witch 3-4 times and every time the witch used to talk to her and made fun of her shortcomings and whenever she came forward to kill her someone came and Anna is saved. And at the end when Anna faces the witch, without taking a second she kills the witch while saying that if you want to kill someone you should kill them without wasting your time by talking to them.

It is very simple, the decisions in bad and difficult situations should be taken quickly, the more you delay the more uncontrollable situations get.

You just have to believe in yourself, that whatever will happen I will handle it. Once your self-confidence is developed then your decision will never be wrong.

Life is a game of reverse bet, no matter how intelligent a person is, it is not necessary that his every decision is correct.

We make decisions for tomorrow based on what is happening today, but in reality, what is going to happen tomorrow is not known to anyone. Today's night may be the last night of your or my life. In this case, our every decision and every plan will be useless but what else can we do?

The time of death is uncertain but tomorrow morning is certain. In this situation, we have to make decisions keeping in mind the certainty.

And the predictability of the uncertain shall be left with that power is better because of who we are in the existence of this universe or this universe is.

No man can be hundred percent correct about anything, a lot of actions or circumstances always have the chance of contrary results. If you look at the events of the second world war, you will find dozens of incidents when a soldier killed his own soldiers unknowingly or the weapons depraved or the bombs thrown on the opponent's side didn't burn. The result was totally against expectations. Look at Hitler, the one who came out with the hope of ruling all over the world, had he ever thought that his decision would be so wrong that eventually, he would have to suicide?

When the decisions of extraordinary people go wrong then the effect and broadness of those decisions are also extraordinary. A decision of the prime minister affects the whole nation whereas a decision taken by a common man affects no one else more than his family. The decisions taken by us affect how many people. We should always keep this thing in mind. Because our life is transient, we should not think it is long even by mistake. We can not make mistakes continuously. Mistakes can happen, but it is necessary to be proven right in some parts, otherwise it will not take time for our life to become hell.

4. learn to lead

If you have big dreams and you aim to live above the common life then you have to develop the capacity of leading. If we tell the simple meaning of leading then it means that it is common for the whole population of 'this world' to have different beliefs and perceptions on every concern.

Instead of forcing your beliefs and perceptions on others, the presence of impugnment between everyone should be finished, and inspiring everyone to walk in one direction is the art of leadership. We can easily see this quality in the owners of big companies, managers, and politicians. Those who do not have the quality of leadership, even if they reach the higher heights won't be able to last there or they might have to suffer loss.

A successful leader has this one quality- politeness. Lack of politeness yields grudges for him from the people working under him and given a chance they will not hesitate in harming him. On the contrary, in the presence of politeness, you will receive love, and people working under you will work with their full efficiency for you.

Because they believe their work will be valued, you care for them. Humans are social and behavioral creatures. Respect-disrespect, love-hate emotions like these are prima facie more affectable than profit-loss. This is the reason that to whom you love or you like, for them, you bear the financial loss whereas for those who you hate you will harm them even if you yourself are suffering from loss.

The second quality is to keep an angle of vision of respect towards the people working for you and not to look at them as unsuccessful, loser, or stupid. If some person comparatively earns less money or is weak then it does not mean that he is stupid or unsuccessful compared to you or you will keep a disrespectful vision towards him. We should always keep one thing in mind: success is very mysterious. If money is the only measure of intelligence then any person who has taken birth in some rich family is worse and foolish than a newborn child because that child has more wealth than others.

A newborn child who isn't even capable enough to eat solid food is actually more lucky than all of us because even though he is a little child, he will have wealth and money many times larger than ours.

That is why it is necessary for one successful leader to have a view of respect towards everyone. Else wealth and success's pride would make him drown. There are several examples available where a father built companies worth millions and the son lost it to the addiction of his ego.

The third quality is the capability of humans to change. If we don't get into religious matters then there are shocking numerous organizations and these followers give more respect to that person as compared to God, the person who has established the organization.

In fact, it is the result of the art of bounding humans are capable of. A successful leader needs to be an expert in this skill and make every person who comes in contact in such a way that a person accepts his leadership. Instead of forcing your opinions on them, other people come around to accepting your opinions by themselves.

This quality can't be taught, rather it is a part of the tendency of other people's way of talking which is present in some and absent in some. Not everyone has the capability to read another person's mind but you can learn and develop this by practicing.

No matter if a person is very intelligent and wise, in the end he is a human. And humans are a set of emotions and thoughts. Yes, some people walk in the opposite streams of nature. You can't win them and neither some psychologist can influence them because you can consider their veritable power more powerful than a nuclear bomb. Think a little bit, today's whole world's existence is based on some underlying reasons from which hunger, thirst, and desires are most important. But when some person starts living above these three things then we can not consider him as common, this is not easy. It is to act free from desires but in real situations, it's hard to win over your own heart. Hence, a successful leader should stay away from these people because they won't accept your subjugation at any cost.

When nature itself couldn't make them walk this path then how can someone else make them change their way of life?

The fourth quality is tolerance. A successful leader needs to have tolerance. Because a lot of the time, they may have to face strong protest as well. Everyone in your team doesn't need to listen to you every time, sometimes you may have to accept their decisions as well. It is important to take care of their needs and feelings, and this is only possible if the leader is tolerant. In absence of this important quality, if you force your decisions onto others then in such a condition it is possible that the people around you will start distancing themselves from you, the smart people will outright leave you and those who are dependent on you will leave after some time. In such a situation you will not have any choice but to walk your path alone. There is a saying, that a lion always walks alone. That's a lie because whenever lions go out to hunt, they go out in a group of four or five. After all, it is only possible to catch prey by grouping up. The reality is that when the animals see a lone lion they gang up like hyenas or wild dogs and attack the lion and kill it. This is the reality of the jungle, thus you must become more tolerant towards the needs and feelings of others. If you don't care about the people associated with you, then they won't care about you either.

9 789393 809421

Printed by Libri Plureos GmbH in Hamburg, Germany